Ruth and Naomi Find Joy After Tragedy

Sylvia Roaché

CONTENTS

DEDICATION

Grace Ann Roaché-Greenidge: With all my love, with all my heart, I treasure you and I honor you. The depth of your character, your boundless love, the joy and companionship we found in each other, will always be cherished. I love you very much.

Mom.

AKNOWLEDGEMENTS

Thanks to my husband Rev. Leonard Roache for his constant encouragement and support.

To Charmaine Curtis for her many hours of typing and helpful assistance in editing. I would not have been able to make my deadline without her help.

To my sisters Amy, Daphne, Millicent and Beryl Bailey my prayer partners.

ABOUT THE BOOK

The book of Ruth is a favorite of many if not most Bible readers. It tells the story of an Israelite family that relocated from Bethlehem, Judah to the country of Moab because of a famine. Unfortunately for Naomi, her husband and two sons all died within a period of ten years.

The widows of the two sons were left with Naomi. Thus we have a trio of widows bathing in bitterness and grief. Naomi blamed God for the tragedies that overwhelmed her. She decides to return to her home in Bethlehem and her two daughters-in-law agreed to go with her.

The three women traveled for a while, then Naomi changed her mind and asked the daughters-in-law to return to their homes in Moab. After many tears, Orpah took Naomi's advice, kissed her goodbye and started on her way back to her home. Ruth then decided that under no circumstance would she leave her mother-in-law. So they both continued the journey to Bethlehem.

Even though this story is centuries old, its message seems quite relevant in our everyday lives with the unexpected tragedies we face. The book of Ruth is beautifully written, and ought to be read by all who have the desire to be inspired. It is a beautiful, romantic story of kindness and its rewards.

Therefore, I have tried to expand my imagination by giving some unrecorded details that I hope will cause my readers to use their imagination as well. The beauty and power of this delightful story is bound to be enjoyed by its readers. I also trust that this book will inspire and refresh those who read it. I hope that you will discover how a God of compassion rewards those who dare to put their trust in him.

THREE OUTSTANDING CHARACTERS

NAOMI

RUTH

BOAZ

WHAT CAN WE LEARN FROM THEM?

CHAPTER 1

THREE OUTSTANDING CHARACTERS

In introducing you to these three outstanding characters in the enchanting book of Ruth, it is important that you spend a few seconds reading the opening verses of the first chapter. By so doing, you will be able to better understand the setting from which Naomi, Ruth and Boaz have come. After you have read these verses you will be asking many questions. These will be questions that most of us have asked and are asking as we face the challenges of life. In the story, answers have been found.

Because this story is so true and similar to the human condition, we will be able to find some answers to some of the questions that our circumstances have created for us contrary to our liking. The caption above these first seven verses is: "Naomi and Ruth" but we need to realize from the start, that although three weddings took place in the story, no romantic account was given until Boaz entered the picture. This is how the story begins:

"In the days when the judges ruled, there was a famine in the land, and a man from Bethlehem in Judah, together with his wife and two sons, went to live for a while in the country of Moab.

The man's name was Elimelech, his wife's name Naomi, and the names of his two sons were Mahlon and Kilion. They were Ephrathites from Bethlehem, Judah. And they went to Moab and lived there.

Now Elimelech, Naomi's husband, died, and she was left with her two sons. They married Moabite women, one named Orpah and the other Ruth. After they lived there about ten years, both Mahlon and Kilion also died, and Naomi was left without her two sons and her husband.

When she heard in Moab that the Lord had come to the aid of his people by providing food for them, Naomi and her daughters-in-law prepared to return home from there. With her two daughters-in-law she left the place where she had been living and set out on the road that would take them back to the land of Judah.

(Ruth 1:1-7 NIV)

From my early teen years, I fell in love with the book of Ruth. I read it over and over and each time I read it I am as enthralled as I was the first time. If you've read this story once, you feel like reading it again. The book of Ruth is a delightful, captivating and romantic story. I have selected the three out-standing characters for us to think about.

Noami, Ruth and Boaz find a place in our hearts that makes us feel that they are very much like we are.

Ray Stedman in his book, "Adventuring Through The Bible," refers to the book of Ruth as the Romance of Redemption. He calls it a literary masterpiece and a beautiful story of a touching romance. He says that it is a book that inflames the imagination because it is entwined with the captivating theme of love, devotion and true romance.

Naomi, Ruth and Boaz show to us the similarity of the human condition. Life is made up of a variety of situations. There are hardships, trials, challenges, sickness, death, grief, bitterness, frustration, determination, falling in love, getting married, having children and having grandchildren. There is also a lesson on the way God works His purpose through the lives of those who put their trust in Him.

Dr. Herbert Lokyer in his book, "All The Books Of The Bible," speaks of the book of Ruth in a beautiful way. This is what he says, "This Hebrew Pastoral idyll is the most perfect, charming and touching narrative in the scripture; and one combining all the traits of human life and character. Of this rare, spiritual gem in the whole realm of literature, Dr. J. Vernon McGee says that it is, 'A love story without using the word love.'"

If you have not read the book of Ruth, you have missed reading an inspiring, uplifting, romantic, captivating, enjoyable and wonderful story. Whether you are a Christian or not, read the book and you will be delighted. It is relaxing and enjoyable to anyone who reads it. The story shows how God uses anyone who is willing to be used to work his purpose out.

His anger lasts only a moment,
his goodness for a lifetime.
Tears may flow in the night,
but joy comes in the morning.
Psalm 30:5 (TEV)

CHAPTER 2

NAOMI PLANS TO RELOCATE

Elimelech, head of the family, became concerned about Naomi his wife, and their two sons. They lived in Bethlehem during a difficult time. There was famine in the country, which made it difficult to obtain food even if you had the money to pay for it.

We can imagine this father and mother of two, sitting and working out a plan to leave their country for a while. They decided to relocate to the country of Moab where there was food. This was not an easy undertaking for Naomi. She would not only be leaving her home, but her community of neighbors, friends, relatives and her place of worship.

Even though it was difficult for Naomi, she had decided with her husband that moving was the right thing to do. Their two sons were young men with friends too, and it was also difficult for them. So Naomi, as mothers do, had to comfort her boys and help to convince them that they would be better off for the move.

I believe that the boys had some questions such as: "Mother, will the neighbors be going on this trip too? How long is the trip going to take? Do we have any family there? How long is the journey going to be? Where are we going to live when we get there?" All these and many more are questions that the boys would be asking and Naomi had to find some answers. The boys were not the only ones that had questions for Naomi.

She had to share the news with neighbors, family and friends, and that was no easy task.

"Naomi, why have you and your husband decided to leave at this time?" some may have asked. "Why couldn't you stay and let us all suffer together? We all cannot leave our house and our property. Why couldn't you and your husband wait until God makes a change in our situation?"

These were hard questions for Naomi. She might have shed a few tears and tried to find answers to all these questions. They may have even tried to impress on her how difficult the move was going to be and maybe she and her husband should think it over before they make the move. Of course, Naomi might have assured them that they were not planning to stay for a long time. They were hoping to return as soon as this scarcity of food was over. Her husband had made up his mind and they would be leaving as soon as they could get themselves ready for the journey.

It wasn't long before Elimelech, Naomi, and their two sons, Mahlon and Kilion packed up their belongings and were ready to say goodbye to all the neighbors, family and friends that they had been sharing their lives with all along. It is never easy to say goodbye to the people you love and care about. I know, because I've had to do it several times and no matter how often you relocate, you always make new friends and neighbors. The last time our family moved neighbors and friends came and helped us to pack our things. They brought food so we wouldn't have to cook. Some brought boxes and wrapping paper, and there was lots of laughter and fun in the house.

Our neighbors across the street brought their camera and we took pictures together in our family room. The couple who lived next door, brought their four children over to say goodbye. The little ones drew pictures with bright colored crayons with words such as: "I love you!" "I will miss you!" and "I don't want you to go." The three year old sat on the stairs beside me and we talked as friends in three year old language and shared a beautiful time. I gave each of them one of the mugs I had in my kitchen so that they would think about us whenever they used them. We can be certain that Naomi did something very different but the feeling was there.

THE JOURNEY TO MOAB

After family and friends met together for a send off party, it is very possible that food was brought and a meal was enjoyed by all. The women no doubt packed some food for the journey. They no doubt went to their place of worship to ask God's help for the trip they were about to take.

There were no RYDER TRUCKS, no U-HAUL and no MOVING VANS. Therefore the neighbors and family, even if they did not feel good about the move, all got together to give a helping hand. Of course Naomi made sure that her husband and sons eliminate all unnecessary baggage by giving away some of their belongings. The animals were loaded. There were hugs and tears and good wishes. It might have been late evening when they started out on their adventurous trip to the country of Moab. They no doubt wanted to start the journey and travel when it was cool.

We are not sure how long the journey was. They would have to stop and rest several times. It was not only necessary for them to rest, it was important that the animals that were carrying the load have some time to rest also. As they continued the journey Naomi may have had some anxious thoughts. After all she and her family were headed to an unknown country. Yes, she had heard that there was available food and that was good, but she had no family or friends. There would be no one to greet them on arrival, but Naomi was a woman of faith and she believed that God would take care of them.

THE ARRIVAL

There is no record as to how Naomi and her family were received by the people of Moab. They did not go there to beg for anything. They did not want to be dependent on them for what they needed. They were responsible and industrious people who did not even wish to relocate. They had left their country only because of the scarcity of food. Elimelech knew he had to take care of his wife and sons, so he went about the business of doing just that. Before long, he had his family settled into what would be home until the famine was over. They missed their loved ones, but they were content to know that they would have enough to sustain then until the famine was over in Bethlehem.

SETTLING IN A NEW PLACE

Although life in the time that this family lived was not as complex as it is in the year 2004, relocating had its challenges. Adjustments had to be made and that is never easy. I often wonder whether the tiresome packing, the tearful parting and long journey is any harder than unpacking, rearranging and finding the things you need when you reach your destination. I imagine that Elimelech walked around the neighborhood and tried to meet and talk with the men. There was a lot to learn in order to adjust to this new life.

As Naomi went about getting her new home in order, she thought about the friends she had left back home. She missed her family and her familiar neighborhood. She recalled some good times and missed what used to be. Now she must settle down, make new friends and continue to pray and hope for the time when she and her family would be returning home.

Naomi was a pleasant person and had no problem meeting her new neighbors. The culture was quite different but this family had a culture of their own. So they lived their culture within a culture like most foreigners do when they relocate to another country. The religion of Moab was idol worship and that was contrary to that of Naomi's family, who worshiped God the Creator. Naomi no doubt shared her faith with some of her friends even though it is not mentioned.

His anger lasts only a moment,
his goodness for a lifetime.
Tears may flow in the night,
but joy comes in the morning.
Psalm 30:5 (TEV)

CHAPTER 3

FAMILY TRAGEDY

There is no reason given why we should believe that Elimelech and his family were not treated well by the Moabites. All seemed to have gone well for a few years. Naomi had made new friends. The young men stayed out of trouble and the family was getting along just fine. But something is about to change that would cast a shadow over the whole picture, something they did not expect.

Elimelech no doubt came home not feeling well one evening. This was very hard for the family. As the days went by he continued to get worse. There is no record as to how long he had been ill. We have only been told that, "Elimelech, Naomi's husband, died, and she was left with her two sons." Naomi was away from her extended family and close friends. This was very hard for her and her sons.

Those who have experienced the loss of a loved one can identify with Naomi's grief. Here she was in a strange country away from family and friends and losing the one closest to her. She had left her home for a better life and now the head of the house- hold dies, leaving her with her two sons. She had not learned to manage without her husband. She had no need to do so. For a while she tried to take comfort in the company of her two sons, but that did not last very long.

One day, Naomi's older son came home and told his mother that he was in love with one of the young ladies of Moab and would like to make her his wife. We are not sure how Naomi felt about her son marrying a young woman from that country, but there wasn't much that she could do to change anything, even if she wanted to. Her son was in love and she felt she should give him her blessing. So not long thereafter, a wedding was planned and a daughter-in-law was brought into the family.

This could have been a difficult time for both Naomi and her daughter-in-law. Naomi had been looking to her sons for comfort and support, but now that her first son had taken unto himself a wife, things would be different. Her daughter-in-law, whose religion was so different from her own, could be a problem. She may have wondered if her son would be so involved with his wife, as he should be, and not be able to give her the attention she needed in her time of grief. She could not be sure, but she decided she would give all the help that she could to her son's wife and befriend her.

Naomi soon found out that she had not just been given a daughter, which she no doubt had wished for when she had her own children, but she now had a friend. After getting acquainted with Naomi, Ruth soon embraced her as a mother and accepted her religion. Ruth had much to learn from her mother-in-law, who was a woman of wisdom. Naomi also learned a lot from Ruth being a younger woman and a native of that country.

They spent many good times together. Ruth was very thoughtful and considerate. So even though she was a newly wed, she paid special attention to her mother-in-law who was grieving for her husband. She decided that she was going to be a good wife and a caring member of the family.

With her husband dying and her older son getting married, Naomi made up her mind to adjust to the changes that had taken place. She had concerns that she was unable to share with anyone. After all her old friends were back home and even though she had made some new ones, she could not share with them what she could with those at home.

Kilion the younger of the two brothers no doubt felt somewhat lonesome after his brother's wedding. His father was no longer with them and his mother was grieving, so he was by himself. Seeing how well his brother was getting along with his lovely wife, he decided that he needed a wife too. We are not certain how soon after his brother's wedding that Naomi had to be involved in another wedding. We are told only that he was married.

Naomi welcomed another daughter-in-law to the family. The young men seemed to be getting along with their wives. Naomi might have grieved even more as she watched her sons enjoying the company of their wives. She was happy for them, of course, but there was no ease from the pain she felt for the loss of her husband. Her daughters-in-law loved her very much and tried to comfort her and she was thankful.

However, the pain would not go away.

We can imagine that during this time, Naomi kept hoping that there would be a grandchild from one of her sons. She may have even teased her daughters-in-law about it. But with all their wishing, none of the women became pregnant. So life went on for a while and they seemed to have been a happy family together except for the constant reminder that a husband and father was missing.

DEATH OF ONE SON

Life has some difficult times for families to go through. No one is ever ready for all the sudden changes that must be faced. Naomi did not expect that her husband would have died before they return to their home in Bethlehem, but he did. So when her son Mahlon became ill, she had all hope that he would get well. Naomi and her daughters-in-law along with their family did all they could to care for him. Inspite of all their efforts Mahlon died.

The sorrow that these women felt can hardly be expressed in words. Naomi must have wondered, "Why is this happening to me? Why is the All Mighty God doing this to me? Am I being punished because I left my homeland? What am I going to do?" As she wept along with her grieving daughter-in-law who is without her young husband, she could not find words that could express the empathy she felt for her. The family was in great mourning.

There is nothing mentioned in the story as to what might have caused the death of Elimelech or his son. Nothing is said about how long after the father's death that his son died. We would like to know how long after the son was married that he became ill. We have no idea how long the sickness lasted and when he died. No such information has been recorded.

There is a proverb that goes like this in the country of Jamaica, "The donkey says, that two troubles are better than one." The donkey is a beast of burden and is used to transport produce from one place to another. Usually there are two hampers, one on each side of the donkey that has to be balanced or the result will be a sore on the back of the animal. At this time in the life of Naomi, it would seem as if one death in her family was not enough. There had to be another to balance the load of grief.

This was a time of great suffering for the three women. Although Orpah had her husband and life seemed to be going well for them, she was still hurting. She was grieving for her beloved father-in-law as well as her brother-in-law. Then there were times when she felt so sorry for Naomi and Ruth. She may have spent as much time as she could, sharing with and comforting them.

While the family was in the throws of grief, Naomi's other son became ill. The mother, wife and sister-in-law did all they could, but day after day Kilion's condition deteriorated. Again we do not know how long his sickness lasted. We are only told that he also died. Neighbors gathered and offered all the help they could give to these three women who had now become widows. Some of the town's people may have wondered why this lovely family had to experience such sorrow? Did they do something to make their God angry with them? What will these three women do?

Joni Eareckson Tada in her Devotional book, DIAMONDS IN THE DUST, in a devotion entitled, "Triple Trouble," asks the question, "Ever heard that old adage, 'Bad things come in threes?'" She mentioned that there is no biblical support for such arithmetic, but it happens. She went on to tell of a time in her life when trouble came to her three times, one after another.

I read Joni's devotion when our family was going through a TRIPLE TROUBLE time. My niece was killed by a man driving under the influence of alchohol in the city of Chicago. Her two young children who were with her in the car had to be air-lifted to the hospital where they remained in a coma for days. They never saw their mother again. A short time after that tragic experience our son died suddenly of a heart attack in Washington, DC. While going through that grief our daughter was diagnosed with breast cancer. We are still enduring the pain of those experiences, and it will be with us for a lifetime in some measure.

Naomi tried to make some sense out of what was

taking place in her life. She had tried to be faithful to her God, so why was this happening to her? She had told her daughters-in-law how good her God was in taking care of those who put their trust in him. Will they have doubts at this time? Her grief had turned to bitterness and she did not know what to do. For how could she comfort her daughters when she was so overcome with bitterness?

His anger lasts only a moment,
his goodness for a lifetime.
Tears may flow in the night,
but joy comes in the morning.
Psalm 30:5 (TEV)

CHAPTER 4

HUMAN SUFFERING

Throughout the Bible there are episodes in which God intervenes in the affairs of humanity. The inescapable and inevitable question is, if the hand of God can be discerned in the workings of human history, why do the righteous suffer, and the wicked prosper? No where in the Bible is this as profound as in the book of Job. God Himself said of Job:

> "There is no one on earth like him; he is blameless and upright, a man who fears God and shuns evil."
>
> (Job 1:8, 2:3)

Job did not only fear God for himself. He had a desire for his children to be God-fearing. His sons took turns to have feasts in their homes to which their sisters were invited. Whenever these times of celebration ended, Job would send and have them purified. Early in the morning he would sacrifice a burnt offering for each of them, thinking, "Perhaps my children have sinned and cursed God in their hearts" This was Job's regular custom. Chapter 1: 4-5. Just because Job was blameless and upright, he was not exempt from suffering. At the heart of the book is the thought that to a mere human the ways of the Creator must remain inscrutable. Job concludes that submission to the Divine Will is the only option really available to him. (George Robinson, "Essential Judaism.")

WHO IS TO BLAME?

The human tendency is to find someone to blame when we are visited by tragedy. Harold Kushner in his book, "Who Needs God?" talks about a bumper sticker he saw which read, "The man who can smile when things are going badly, has just thought of someone to blame it on."

To have lost the three significant persons in her life so quickly one after the other, Naomi in her grief felt she had to find out the reason why all this sorrow had been placed on her. In her search to find an answer, she could find nothing. She could not blame her husband or her sons for they had nothing to do with their death. She could not blame her two daughters-in-law who were sharing the same grief. So she decided it had to be God. She did not feel she could argue with Him, so she became bitter and told her daughters-in-law: "It is more bitter for me than for you, because the Lord's hand has gone out against me." (Ruth 1:13)

Those who have experienced the loss of a loved one can try to identify with Naomi's pain. When she left her home in Bethlehem for the country of Moab, she was known as a pleasant person. The very meaning of her name is pleasantness. Now she is bitter and has no one to blame but the God she served and expected to protect her from trouble. Would her daughters-in-law believe in the God she introduced to them? Are they wondering to themselves, "If Naomi's God is the true God, why did he allow all this grief to come to her?" Naomi felt forsaken at this time.

When at midnight I received the call telling of my niece's death (who was like a daughter to me), I was numb. I was angry too but my anger was toward the young man who got behind the wheel of his car while intoxicated. To express some of the anger I felt, I wrote a letter to the young man whom I had never met. I expressed to him all the people his lack of responsibility had hurt. I expressed to him how our large family had to travel long distances to be together. I asked him to try and imagine the thousands of dollars that had to be spent for plane fares and other transportation, hotels and food. Some family members came from other countries. Some had to take time off their jobs without pay. I mentioned doctors and hospital bills, funeral costs and the children who after coming out of a coma, if they did, would never see their mother again. I tried to think of every hardship this senseless act brought to our family.

My letter was never sent to that young man. But it gave me the opportunity to express some of my anger. I began to think of the sorrow he brought to his own family, especially his parents and siblings. Unlike Naomi, I could find someone to blame.

When at midnight my brother-in-law brought the news to us that our son had passed away suddenly with a heart attack, I'm not sure it was anger. I didn't have anyone to blame. I just kept hitting my brother-in-law as if he had done something wrong and I was given the right to hit him. He tried to hold me as I kept hitting him on his shoulder. It was his daughter who was killed by the drunk driver. So he said he understood because it was like living his experience all over again.

FAMILY AND FRIENDS

Family and friends are wonderful to have around in times of grief. They sit quietly with you, they cry when you cry and if you can manage to take time for a smile, they are there with you too. My sisters' (who loved our son as if he were their own), would recall some of the happy times he shared with them. They would recall the laughter and fun shared at family gatherings. We talked and laughed about the foods he liked and those he didn't like. Some would recall the times spent around the piano singing while he played. We look at pictures together with mixed emotions.

Friends would call from distant cities just at the time we needed to hear from some caring person. Because of the love shown to us by family and friends, we became more aware of God's love and care as we continued to read and believe His word. In the midst of all the consolation of family and friends and our unwavering faith in God, there is an underlying ache that can hardly be fully expressed.

Death is so final and there is nothing we can do to change it. It is no wonder that Naomi felt as though she was being punished. She had left home with her husband and two sons. On returning home she would leave behind three graves. In all of her grief and pain not one of her extended family from her homeland was present to grieve with her. She felt alone and bewildered.

She felt she had been given more than her share of grief.

NAOMI'S GRIEF

Naomi felt devastated. She felt as though every reason for happiness was taken from her. She felt she had no reason to even hope. She was depressed even though deep in her heart she knew she had been faithful to God and she could trust Him still. It is just that we, with our finite minds cannot fully understand an infinite God. Naomi must have felt like the writer of the psalm when he wrote:

When I kept silent, my bones wasted away through my groaning all day long. For day and night your hand was heavy upon me; my strength was sapped as in the heat of summer.
(Psalm 32:3-4)

Naomi felt a pain that can be understood only by those who have gone through similar experiences. Her two daughters-in-law had lost their husbands too, but their grief was not the same. She had lost them all. She felt lonely and sad.

A PUPPY

I went through the check out counter and sat on a bench in front of the grocery store. I was waiting for my sister who was checking out her grocery. At the other end of the bench, was a lady with a cute fluffy white puppy. She kept stroking it as she held it close to her chest. "That's a real cute puppy." I said as I moved a bit closer to her. She was delighted that I noticed what seemed to be her special treasure. She smiled as she held the small pup close to her face.

"This is my very special little friend. My granddaughter gave it to me a few weeks ago when my husband passed away. She knew how much I would be missing him, so she bought me this puppy to keep me company."

"Oh, I'm so sorry to hear that your husband passed away. I imagine you do miss him. But I'm glad to know that you have a thoughtful and caring granddaughter. It was lovely of her to give you such an adorable puppy."

"Yes, my granddaughter is such a dear. We love each other a lot and I do love my little friend here."

Remembering how comforting that tiny pup is to that grandmother, I can't help thinking how much better Naomi might have felt if some one had given her a puppy. But God is faithful and in all of this grief that His daughter is going through, she will one day discover that He has a plan for her life. She will receive a gift far better than a puppy.

His anger lasts only a moment,
his goodness for a lifetime.
Tears may flow in the night,
but joy comes in the morning.
Psalm 30:5 (TEV)

CHAPTER 5

NAOMI'S RETURN TO BETHLEHEM

Naomi felt her pain becoming almost unbearable. She kept thinking about returning to her extended family in Bethlehem. She tried to find some semblance of hope and comfort in Moab but she was getting homesick. The thought of returning home brought mixed feelings. How could she return alone with nothing to show for the ten years she had been away? The family left for Moab in order to get food to preserve their lives. They found food. Her two sons found beautiful girls to marry, but now she is going home leaving the bodies of her husband and two sons, buried in the land she had hoped would have sustained them.

How was she going to face her family and friends, especially those who did not agree with their plan to move? Would they accuse her of turning away from the God she served before she left? Would they think that the family did something terribly wrong, and God was punishing her for it? After all, in her heart she felt that God had something to do with all the grief she was experiencing. She could not say why, but she felt He was to blame.

Naomi was perplexed. But somehow she got news that God had provided food for His people in Judah. She could go home but how would Ruth and Orpah feel about her leaving them. They had been so good and kind to her in all of her time with them. Again I believe that Naomi felt like Job when he said:

> "My eyes have grown dim
> With grief; my whole frame
> Is but a shadow."
> (Job 17:7)

A FAMILY CONFERENCE

Naomi finally made up her mind. She would call her daughters-in-law and together they would have a family conference. Then again, fearing how the women would respond, Naomi thought that maybe she should just stay with them until she dies and be buried with her husband and her sons. There were many questions, many doubts and fears, but the family conference was planned.

Naomi called the women together and they sat down together as she began to share with them what she had been thinking about. She explained to them about the good news she had heard that God had provided food for his people in Bethlehem. She hated to leave them but she had to go. The discussion turned out easier than Naomi thought. Both her daughters-in-law thought it was a good idea. So they decided to go with her. We can imagine how eager they were to share the news with their families. They may have been excited to be going to a different country, especially with their beloved mother-in-law.

After getting their plans together, they agreed on a time when they would leave and started packing. We are not sure about the mode of transportation. They may have had a couple of animals to help carry their belongings.

THE JOURNEY BEGINS

The three widows executed their plans for the journey. They said goodbye to their family and friends. That evening before starting the journey, we can imagine all three of them making a last visit to the resting place of their husbands. They made their plans and decided to start the journey very early in the morning. All seemed to have been going quite well, but Naomi was doing some hard thinking. Being the thoughtful mother that she was, she began to have second thoughts. She wondered to herself, how these young women would fare in the strange country they were going to.

NAOMI CHANGES HER MIND

Before they had gone very far on the journey, Naomi began to rethink her plan. She took occasional glances at her two beautiful daughters-in-law. She tried to think of the kind of life they would have in her country. After all, the people of Moab were not known to be friends of the people in Judah. How are these young women going to fit into this new culture? How would they be supported? She had extended family but they were strangers. They were also young women and she was not. Both of these young women were widows.

The life of widows during the time these women lived was not good. "Widows were taken advantage of or ignored. They were almost always poverty stricken. God's law therefore provided that the nearest relative of the dead husband should take care of the widow. But Naomi had no relative in Moab and she did not know if any of her relatives were alive in Israel." (Life Application Bible)

We can presume that Naomi did not think it was a good idea that two other widows should return home with her. She loved her two daughters-in-law and did not wish to see them hurt any more than they were.

We do not know how far the three women had gone on the journey. Naomi decided that she needed to share with them what she had been thinking about before they went any further. So she no doubt came to a cool shade tree and suggested that they stop for a little while. Ruth and Orpah tried to keep a happy conversation going but Naomi hinted that she wanted to share something with them. They both looked at her and waited to hear what she had to say. Naomi hesitated for a while trying to decide the best way to explain what was on her mind. Then to the astonishment of her daughters-in-law she said:

"Go back each of you to your mother's

home. May the Lord show kindness to you,
as you have shown to your dead and to me.
May the Lord grant that each of you will find
rest in the home of another husband."

(Ruth 1: 8-9)

The young women were surprised and felt very
sad that Naomi had changed her mind. They
couldn't understand why the change of plans. They
had all talked about the matter. They had made up
their minds for the move. Why is this happening to
them now?

Naomi moved closer to them and hugged and
kissed them goodbye. When she did that, they
protested. "We will go back with you to your
people." They both insisted that they would go with
her as they had planned. Naomi was firm in her decision and they knew that she was. So they did not just
shed a few tears they cried out loud. They had said
goodbye to their father-in-law. They had said goodbye to both their husbands. Naomi was all they had
left as a link to the ones they had loved and lost and
now she is telling them not to go with her as they
had planned.

Naomi was not enjoying this either. So she
decided to spend some time reasoning with them.
She explained to them that she was never going to
have any more sons that could become their
husbands. She even called them her daughters,
making them feel even more loved than they knew
they were. She told them that she was too old to have
children and even if it were possible for her to get a

husband and have sons, she didn't think that they would wait around until they were grown and could become husbands for them. This was some good reasoning. Therefore the young women took some time to think about what they should do.

ORPAH RETURNED HOME

We know very little about Orpah. She was the wife of Kilion, Naomi's son. Naomi spoke well of her when she asked her to return to her people. She had been a good wife and a caring daughter-in-law just as Ruth was. She had made up her mind to go back home with Naomi and continue to be a part of her life. Naomi was very persuasive with her sugges-tion, but it was not easy for them to change their minds again. Orpah thought about what her mother-in-law suggested. "Maybe, mother is right after all. Maybe she is thinking that her people may not like us and she wouldn't want us to be uncomfortable."

Orpah could have reasoned that her mother-in-law loved them very much. She had no doubt about that. She loved her too. But Naomi was older and at the moment was still overwhelmed with grief. More grief could be added to her life if they could not take care of themselves in a strange country. Orpah might have thought that it was foolish to continue, since according to Naomi, there was really nothing to look forward to.

Orpah agreed that Naomi was right when she said she was too old to have children. She could understand all of Naomi's reasoning. Therefore she must decide whether to take a chance and go on with her or go back to her country. It was a difficult decision to make in such a short time. If she decides to go back home she needed to do so before going any further on the journey. She had no one to consult for advice. She had to make up her own mind and it was not easy.

Naomi made another plea by saying, "It is more bitter for me than for you, because the Lord's hand has gone out against me." There was another time of weeping.

All three women were very sad. After listening to the convincing, yet loving words from Naomi, Orpah through much tears, gave her mother-in-law a tender embrace, kissed her goodbye and walked away in sadness.

Many thoughts crowded Orpah's mind: Am I doing the right thing? Am I saying a final goodbye to the two women who have become a part of my life? I will miss being with them in grief as well as in times of laughter. She walked for a while, then she sat by the wayside thinking and weeping. She felt like going back to talk with Naomi and Ruth. Maybe they are missing her and wouldn't mind if she came along after all.

Then she thought, "what will my folks think about me returning home?" Would they welcome her or would they think she did the wrong thing. After sitting, thinking and crying for a while, she decided to return to her people whatever the outcome would be.

Naomi and Ruth watched Orpah as she kept going but looking back and waving at them. She had taken the instructions of her mother-in-law and was on her way back to join her family. Naomi was sad to see her go and yet she felt that she had done the right thing. She took her eyes off Orpah and turned to Ruth who was still standing beside her. She decided she needed to give Ruth a few more words of encouragement. "Look," she said, " Your sister-in-law is going back to her people and her god. Go back with her."

(Ruth 1:15) Even though she feared taking the journey by herself, Naomi tried to be firm in her speech.

Ruth listened to the persuasive words of Naomi, but she had something to say also. While Naomi had been instructing her and Orpah, Ruth was silently asking herself some hard questions. What would her dead husband think if he could see them? Just how would he feel if the wife he loved and cared for would leave his grieving mother to go that journey by herself? How could she live with herself? Would she be able to sleep at nights not knowing what happened to the woman who had been a mother and a friend to her? She must have thought, " My heart is fixed. My mind is made up and I'm going to let her know just how I feel."

Ruth respectfully listened to the mother who meant the world to her. When she was through speaking, Ruth might have wiped away the tears from her eyes with the corner or her shawl. Then placing both hands on Naomi's shoulders and look-ing straight in her eyes, she conveyed to her the depth of her unflinching resolve. I believe in her heart she was saying. " Listen to me mother and

listen good. I'm going to speak my mind and I want
you to know from the start that I have no intention of
changing my mind. When I started this journey, I
decided to go all the way and nothing is going to
stop me. Now here is what I have to say to you:

> "Don't urge me to leave you or to turn back from you.
> Where you go I will go, and where you stay I will stay.
> Your people will be my people and your God my God.
> Where you die I will die, and there I will be buried.
> May the Lord deal with me, be it ever so severely,
> If anything but death separates you and me.
> (Ruth 1: 16)

Naomi listened to Ruth's declaration of her
resolve and it was so convincing, she was speechless. She must have thought, " I knew Ruth was a
great daughter-in-law, but I never thought she was
such a woman of stature and determination. I believe
they embraced each other again and this time there
were no tears. Ruth's love and devotion for her
mother-in-law was undaunted. She loved and
respected Naomi. She no doubt had taken many
good instructions from her. But this admonition to
change her mind about going on this journey with
her was one she had no intention of taking.

The perplexity, pain and fear that Ruth felt when
Naomi asked her to return to her homeland all
subsided. She did not wonder about whether or not
she would be accepted in Naomi's culture. She had
decided that whatever the future brought to her she
was determined to face the challenge. All she prayed

for now was that the God she had learned to depend on would give her the needed strength. Her mother-in-law who taught her to trust in God was bitter at this time. Ruth understood it was because of the overwhelming grief that she was experiencing. Ruth had a compassionate and understanding heart and would not focus on Naomi's seeming lack of faith at this trying time.

Ruth's words to Naomi were comforting to say the least. Two hearts were now drawn together as never before. Naomi must have thought, "Here is the daughter I never had." She never thought she would have heard those words from anyone. How could Ruth find this kind of love and devotion to bestow on her when she was also grieving? In her heart, Naomi must have thought, "Where did my son find this gem to bequeath to his mother?"

It is a great feeling when love and devotion are expressed in the language that Ruth used in this tender moment with her mother-in-law. I remember some years ago while visiting with my daughter and her family; she was delighted that I was spending some time with her. As we sat on the front porch of her house she said, "Mom, I want you and Dad to know that if the time ever comes when you both need me, there is no job that I wouldn't give up to come and take care of you." I hoped then that she would never have to make that sacrifice, but to hear her express her love for us in that manner spoke volumes. And I do believe that Naomi experienced what I felt.

His anger lasts only a moment,
his goodness for a lifetime.
Tears may flow in the night,
but joy comes in the morning.
Psalm 30:5 (TEV)

CHAPTER 6

THE JOURNEY

After Ruth declared her unquestionable decision, there was no room for any other instruction from her mother-in-law. The case was closed. Now that all this talk is over, it's time to hit the road. The only words that might have been said at this time would be, "Come on mother, let's go. We have a long journey ahead of us."

There is something dynamic about a made-up mind. We will never achieve unless we make up our minds about what we want to accomplish. It is also good for us to state our intention, speak so others can hear it. Speak it so you can hear yourself saying it and you will be aware of the challenges you have to face, and try to find what it will take to make it happen.

After Ruth declared her intention in such strong language, her mother-in-law heard and believed her. Ruth also knew in her heart that there would be difficult times ahead, but whatever she had to face, she was ready. She had nothing more to verbally express to Naomi. From now on it was going to be love in action.

As the two women continued the journey, there was much to talk about. Naomi had been on the road before but it was a new experience for Ruth. Naomi no doubt pointed out the things that had changed. After all, she had been on that road ten years ago and things do change. She might have pointed out some of the rest stops and used them when they were tired. I believe they had a wonderful time together. Naomi also realized that she needed Ruth with her, and Ruth was delighted to be going home with her mother-in-law who had become such a vital part of her life.

They traveled for a while, then they stopped and rested at intervals. Ruth no doubt kept watch over her mother while she slept. Even though Naomi was the mother in title and love, Ruth was playing the role at this time. She had made up her mind to take care of her mother, watch over her, and make sure that all would go well.

We can imagine that the journey became less tiresome as the two women walked and talked. Ruth had many questions to ask Naomi about culture as well as her extended family. When Naomi expressed the pain of returning without her husband and two sons, Ruth would always speak words of hope and comfort to her.

His anger lasts only a moment,
his goodness for a lifetime.
Tears may flow in the night,
but joy comes in the morning.
Psalm 30:5 (TEV)

CHAPTER 7

ARRIVAL IN BETHLEHEM

Naomi and Ruth traveled together until they arrived in Bethlehem. They were tired from the long journey and the marks of grief could be seen on their faces, especially Naomi. Ruth was young and beautiful but she was a stranger. No one knew her, but they remembered who Naomi was. They recalled how beautiful she looked when she said goodbye to them ten years before. She had left with her husband and her two sons. Now she returns without them and is accompanied by this beautiful young woman. No wonder the whole town was stirred because of them. The people looked on in wonder. They thought this woman looked like Naomi but was that really the Naomi they knew? There was such a change in her appearance, the women exclaimed, "Can this be Naomi?"

This was a very sad time for Naomi. She was not only overcome with grief, but now when she should be welcomed home with warm greetings, everyone stood staring at her and wondering what had happened to her. She even felt unworthy of the name she grew up with and loved. She was bitter and wanted them to know that she felt as if the God she served faithfully was punishing her. Therefore, she said to them as they looked on in wonder:

"Don't call me Naomi, (which means, pleasant). Call me Mara, (which means bitter) because the Almighty has made my life very bitter. I went away full, but the Lord has brought me back empty. Why call me Naomi? The Lord has afflicted me; the Almighty Has brought misfortune upon me."

(Ruth 1: 20-21)

Ruth stood by and listened to her overwhelmed mother-in-law. She gave her all the support that she could. Naomi introduced her to the women and told them how wonderful a wife she had been to her son. She also told them how she had left her family and friends and had come to live with her. Best of all she was now serving the true God that they worshiped. Some of the women embraced her and made her feel welcome. They were very tired. Naomi's family helped them to get settled in her home that she had left ten years before. Neighbors, family and friends did whatever they could to comfort Naomi. They were touched by the fact that Ruth had left her family, friends and country in order to take care of her mother-in-law.

Naomi and Ruth were not able to travel with all

of the things they owned. They may have had to leave most of their belongings. They could not travel with much so they were destitute. But they were glad that the journey was over.

Naomi was very tired and very sad. She spent some time talking with Ruth but she felt the need for rest. She was very depressed. Coming back to her empty house was difficult and seemed unbearable. She felt like a failure. Life seemed empty without her husband and her two sons. Falling asleep was not easy for her. She felt weak and helpless.

Ruth was tired too and was dealing with the loss of her own husband. She had moments of tears and sadness, not only for herself, but also for her mother-in-law and her sister-in-law Orpah who had returned to her people. Ruth wondered if she would ever see her again. But she also had some important matters in mind that she had to deal with. Therefore she began to think of what she could do in order to provide for her mother-in-law and herself.

RUTH GOES TO WORK

Ruth could have decided not to have anything to do with her mother-in-law. She had been married to her son who was now dead and she had no children with him. She could have said, "Let her go her way and I'll go mine." But instead she chose to stay close to her grieving mother and pledged to take care of her as long as she lived.

Therefore, on their return to Bethlehem, Ruth's first concern was finding a way to work and support her mother-in-law. Naomi knew the town. Ruth did not, but she was strong and healthy. She too had suffered grief and was hurting. Naomi had suffered three times as much, and was older. Ruth's idea was not to help her mother-in-law find something to do. She would go alone. She would trust the providence of the God she had chosen to serve.

Ruth had no resume or recommendation from any former employer. She had no idea where to turn. She did not know if she would be laughed at, refused or denied. She did not concentrate on rejection. She would go against all odds, face any obstacle. Her mind was made up. She decided to go out alone without a friend or guide, but with faith and determination, trusting God to work things out for her.

From all appearances, Ruth was an industrious young woman. She was not going to sit by and wait for the people of Bethlehem to show pity on her or her mother-in-law. She would be happy to take a job if she could find one, but where could she go? She was a stranger. No one knew her but Naomi; whose spirit at that time was so broken. She could not think as at other times. We can imagine how distressing this was to Ruth.

Ruth felt very strange in this new environment and hardly knew what to make of it. Many of us can identify with her. We have been in strange places where we knew no one and no one knew us. We were faced with challenges that we had never experienced before. We had to face challenges that seem almost impossible. When you find yourself in a new community, you stay alert. You listen to what people are saying. You listen to friends meeting and greeting each other. In so doing, you gather information that can help you.

Ruth was paying attention and she heard people making plans and talking about a harvest. Ruth was going to find a way to support her mother-in-law and her mind was at work trying to think of something that she could do. She may have wondered if she could find a job reaping barley, but workers were already hired and maybe they wouldn't hire her anyway. She kept on thinking and remembered that she had declared to Naomi in no uncertain terms that she would stand by her side. She had affirmed her that they would face all of the challenges of life together. They were going to be a family. They would share their joys as well as their pain. She meant it when she said, "Your people shall be my people and your God my God."

His anger lasts only a moment,
his goodness for a lifetime.
Tears may flow in the night,
but joy comes in the morning.
Psalm 30:5 (TEV)

CHAPTER 8

LAW OF GLEANING

I do believe that Ruth engaged her mother-in-law in serious conversation after they had rested a while. They were tired after the long journey, but the harvest was in progress and that was the only place Ruth thought she might find something to do. So as they discussed the matter, Naomi gave Ruth some lessons in the new religion she had embraced.

Under the laws of Moses, gleaning was allowed for widows as well as for strangers and the poor, "When you are harvesting in your field and you overlook a sheaf, do not go back to get it. Leave it for the alien, the fatherless and the widow, so that the Lord your God may bless you in all the work of your hands. When you beat the olives from your trees, do not go back over the branches a second time. Leave what remains for the alien, the fatherless and the widow. When you harvest grapes in your vineyard, do not go over the vines again, Leave what remains for the alien, the fatherless and the widow. Remember that you were slaves in Egypt. That is why I command you to do this." (Deuteronomy 24:19-22)

After Ruth heard about the law of gleaning after reapers, she gave some serious thought about the idea. She knew that she qualified as a widow and an alien. She had to do something in order to support her mother-in-law and herself. Friends and neighbors were kind and brought food to them, but Ruth knew that wouldn't last for long. She had to find a way to be self-sufficient. Now that she had thought it through, she said to Naomi, "Let me go to the fields and pick up the leftover grain behind anyone in whose eyes I find favor." (Ruth 2:2) Naomi gave her permission to go ahead.

RUTH'S HUMBLE SPIRIT

Ruth had the agreement of her mother-in-law therefore she prepared herself for the adventure. She got ready, said goodbye to Naomi, not knowing in whose field she would be favored to glean. Naomi wished her well and told her to be careful. She watched her as she hurried along until she was out of sight. How she wished things were different so Ruth would not have to go out like that. She prayed for Ruth and felt a deep love for her.

As Ruth hurried along, she had some apprehensions. There were fears and doubts. Even if you are a qualified person taking a job for the first day, there can be feelings of fear and suspicion. You wonder if you will be able to do the job well? What kind of people will you be working with? Will they like you or will you like them? These and many more questions enter our minds on that first day on the job.

Ruth had to deal with a lot of questions. She was a stranger. She was not going to start a job for the first day. She was not going to work for a salary. She was going to pick up what reapers dropped if they would let her. According to the explanation Naomi gave her, she knew she qualified to glean, but where will she find a place? Whatever happened, she would be among people she didn't know. The sun was going to be very hot. She thought about her husband and missed him very much. Without much thinking, she felt the warm tears trickling down her cheeks. How she wished she didn't have to go looking for work. She dried her tears and remembered the promise she made to her mother-in-law and kept going. Ruth did not accommodate any negative thoughts. Yes, at this time of her life she was poor, but she was not going to act the part. Whichever field she was permitted to glean in, she would remember that she was there with a purpose. Her beloved mother-in-law would not be hungry as long as she was able to glean after the reapers.

RUTH ASKS PERMISSION

Ruth watched the laborers as they went to the fields. She followed at a distance and tried to decide which field she would ask permission to enter. She focused on one group of workers and followed them to the farm that they were going to. She watched and listened as they got their assignment from the foreman. Somehow in her heart she wished that she was one of them, but she was not there to ask for a job. She was a stranger, she was a widow and a Moabitess.

It is a terrible feeling when someone knows that they are looked upon as inferior to those around them.

I believe this was extremely painful for Ruth. She was once the respected wife of Naomi's son. She was loved in her country. She could have remained there. Even though she had started out with Naomi, she could have returned with her sister-in-law, when Naomi tried to persuade her to do so. Now here she was feeling as if she had butterflies in her stomach. She scolded herself for thinking those thoughts and as the last worker was assigned, she knew she had to act right away.

She politely greeted the foreman as she hurried to where he was standing."My name is Ruth. I am the daughter-in-law of Naomi. I have returned with her from Moab and will be living with her so that she will not have to be alone. I want to be able to take care of her. I don't know very much about this country, but I was told that I might be allowed to pick up droppings that fall from your reapers. If you would be so kind, I respectfully ask that I be given the privilege to glean after your reapers today, so that I'll have something for my mother-in-law and me."

Ruth was so beautiful and spoke with such dignity, the foreman was more than willing to respond positively. After getting instruction as to where she could go and what she should do, she thanked him and hurried off to get started. She decided to work as fast as she could since that was the only day's work she was sure of.

His anger lasts only a moment,
his goodness for a lifetime.
Tears may flow in the night,
but joy comes in the morning.
Psalm 30:5 (TEV)

CHAPTER 9

RUTH'S FIRST DAY
AT WORK

It does not take a lot of imagination to understand how Ruth felt at the end of her first day at work in this new country. This day seemed to be the most exciting day in her life. Because of the circumstances, this day was more exciting than her wedding day. This day was a unique day when for the first time she could feel the touch of God's own hand on her life, and there is no experience to compare. Those who have felt this unexplainable joy can understand.

She gathered all her bundles of wheat and barley and settled down and threshed out all that she had gleaned. She had an ephah, about a half a bushel, which was enough to feed herself and her mother-in-law for about five days. She was pleased with what she had accomplished. As she gathered her belongings together, she said goodbye to those she had gleaned after and started on her way back home.

Ruth hurried to greet her mother-in-law, who had

been praying and waiting for her to return home.
Naomi was surprised at the unusually large amount of
grain that she brought home. Ruth quickly gave her
the portion of her lunch that she had saved for her.
Seeing the glow in Ruth's eyes and the happy smile
on her face, Naomi knew that she had good news to
share with her. Observing the ample supply of grain
that she brought in, the food she brought for her
dinner, she knew that someone had done her a special
favor, and she could hardly wait to hear who it was.

Of course, Ruth had a lot to tell, but she was
enjoying watching Naomi savor the food she had
brought. In a little while, she would be sharing the
joy. Naomi could not wait. The suspense was a bit
more than she could take at the moment. So as she
started to eat and enjoy the first taste of the good
food, she asked, "Daughter, where have you gleaned
today? And where did you work? Blessed be the one
who took notice of you!" (Ruth 2:19)

Well, Ruth was delighted to oblige. Her response
was one of joy beyond expression. To put her experience in our words, this is what she might have said,
"Oh mother, I had a most delightful and blessed day.
I went to this field and I felt real fearful. I was so
scared for a while. I didn't know anyone. So I waited
as I observed a gentleman who was giving orders to
the workers. I felt that he was the one in charge. So
when he was through giving the assignments, I went
to him and asked if he could please allow me to pick
up droppings that fell from the reapers.

I told him that I am your daughter-in-law who

came back from Moab with you. He showed me where the young women were harvesting and told me I could go and follow them. I thanked him and hurried to where the young women were reaping. I worked very hard and took just a short rest from the sun. I was trying to get as much done for the day because I was not sure if I could go back there tomorrow."

RUTH MEETS BOAZ

Ruth continued to tell Naomi about the most exciting part of her day. She was following along and picking up the stalks that dropped from the hands of the reapers when she heard a strong voice that shouted to all the workers, "May the Lord be with you!" Then all the workers answered, "May the Lord bless you!" Ruth stopped her gleaning and looked to see who it was. She told Naomi that she saw this tall venerable gentleman standing as he glanced over the field. She soon found out that he was the owner of the farm. She had never heard such a wonderful exchange between a boss and his employees.

I do believe Ruth wished she was one of the workers and had a boss as pleasant as the gentleman seemed to be. She bent down again and reminded herself of the reason she was there. While she was working, the gentleman whose name was Boaz, noticed this strange, beautiful young woman in the field. So he asked the foreman, "Whose young woman is that?" The foreman told him that she was the young woman who came back from Moab with Naomi. She had asked if she could be permitted to glean after the reapers. The foreman told Boaz that she had been working steadily, except when she took a short break. Ruth had no idea that this exchange was taking place.

Ruth kept working when suddenly she heard footsteps behind her. She lifted her head, looked around and saw Boaz coming toward her. Her heart skipped a beat and she didn't know what to think. He stopped as he got close to her, introduced himself and continued to speak. "My daughter, listen to me. Don't go and glean in another field and don't go away from here. Stay here with my servant girls. Watch the field where the men are harvesting, and follow along after the girls. I have told the men not to touch you, and whenever you are thirsty, go get a drink from the water jars the men have filled."

As Ruth tried to tell this wonderful news to her mother-in-law, she felt as though she was floating on air. She thought she was having a dream, but it was all very real. Then she said to Naomi, "Mother, you can't imagine how I felt when this kind gentleman spoke to me and even invited me to have lunch with him. I bowed down with my face to the ground and asked him, why had I found favor with him seeing I am a stranger and do not have the standing of one of his servant girls? He told me that he had been told how good I had been to you and how I had left my country to make my home with you in this strange country."

Ruth continued with her joyful news. She had hoped that her situation would change at some future time, but she never thought it would be this way. She explained to Naomi that Boaz complimented her on the love she had shown her. He also pronounced a blessing upon her when he said, "May the Lord repay you for what you have done .May you be richly rewarded by the Lord, the God of Israel, under whose wings you have come to take refuge." (Ruth 2: 12)

Naomi was overjoyed. Her face looked as though she had had a makeover. Ruth saw a mother-in-law whose faith came alive before her eyes. I do believe that Naomi stood to her feet with hands lifted above her head with a voice Ruth had not heard before.

Hearing that the name of the man in whose field she worked was Boaz, Naomi exclaimed:

"The Lord bless him! He has not stop show-ing his kindness to the living and the dead. That man is a close relative; he is one of our Kinsman-redeemers."

(Ruth 2: 20)

KINSMAN-REDEEMER

This was Ruth's chance to understand who a kinsman-redeemer was. We can imagine how ready Naomi was to explain it all to her. So she proceeded to educate her daughter-in-law in one of the most important customs of the new country she had adopted as her own. "A kinsman-redeemer is a rela-tive who volunteers to take responsibility for the extended family. When a woman's husband dies, the law provides that she can marry a brother of her dead husband." (Deut. 25: 5) If there is not a brother, the nearest relative to the deceased husband could become a kinsman-redeemer and marry the widow.

The nearest relative did not have to marry the widow. If he chose not to, the next nearest relative could take his place. If no one chose to help the widow, she would probably live in poverty the rest of her life, because in Israelite culture, the inheritance was passed on to the son or nearest relative, not to the wife. To take the sting out of these inheritance rules, there were laws for gleaning and kinsman-redeemer. (Life Application Bible, Tindale House Publishers, Inc.)

Hope springs once more in the life of Naomi. We can imagine that Ruth listened carefully to the many things Naomi taught her. She had many questions in her mind, but she did not ask at this time. She had gone to the field to glean after the reapers so that there would be food for her and her mother-in-law. Therefore, she was going to keep working to that end.

Naomi recalled that Ruth said Boaz told her to stay in his field close to the working girls. As she thought about it, she decided to add some reinforcement to the idea. "It will be good for you my daughter, to go with his girls, because in someone else's field you might be harmed." (Ruth 2: 22)

RUTH'S WORK TO THE END OF HARVEST

Ruth and her mother-in-law continued to live and share life together. Day after day, Ruth got up early and made her way to the field. She stayed with the women as she was instructed to do until the last day of harvest. She felt good that she and her

mother-in-law were together and she had been able
to obtain food that would sustain them for a while.
Industrious as Ruth was, she might have been thinking of finding something else to do. But Naomi was
coming alive again and her mind was ticking away
like a clock. She was not feeling as sad and bitter as
she did before. She saw that God had not forgotten
her. He had opened a wonderful door of opportunity
to her daughter-in-law who meant so much to her.
Naomi decided it was time for her to act and help
Ruth to enter this open door.

His anger lasts only a moment,
his goodness for a lifetime.
Tears may flow in the night,
but joy comes in the morning.
Psalm 30:5 (TEV)

CHAPTER 10

NAOMI'S PLAN

One day, Naomi decided to put into action what she had been thinking about. She was delighted that Ruth was with her and that they cared so much about each other. Naomi was an unselfish person. She might have been content with her widowhood, but Ruth was a beautiful, energetic young woman. That is why Naomi had insisted that she and her sister-in-law return to their homeland and hopefully they would find husbands who would make a home for them.

Ruth had decided to make the journey with Naomi, and pledged to spend her life with her. Therefore, Naomi felt that she should do all she could to make a better life for them. Ruth was not only her daughter-in-law she was also her friend. One day Naomi said to her:

"My daughter, should I not try to find a home for you where you will be provided for?" Is not Boaz with whose servant girls you have been, a kinsman of ours? Tonight he will be winnowing barley on the threshing floor. Wash and perfume yourself, and put on your best clothes. Then go down to the threshing floor, but don't let him know you are there until he has finished eating and drinking. When he lies down, note the place where he is lying. Then go and uncover his feet and lie down. He will tell you what to do.

(Ruth 3: 1-5)

NAOMI SHIFTS HER FOCUS

Ruth had worked tirelessly in the field of Boaz along with his servant girls. Now the harvest was over and she could rest for a while. She was content to know that there was enough food to sustain her and her beloved mother-in-law. She no doubt felt a sense of peace. She could now spend some time exploring and learning about the new environment, the culture, and the God she had embraced and who had begun to show His hand of blessing in her life. She could now take time to reflect on her past, enjoy the present and dream of a brighter future.

Even as Ruth was settling down in her new location, Naomi's mind was at work in a new way. Realizing that Boaz could act as a kinsman-redeemer, she began to make plans for the redemption of Ruth's inheritance, which belonged to her by virtue of her marriage to Elimelech's son Mahlon. Naomi had shifted her focus from her grief and bitterness at this time.

After experiencing the love shown to her by her

adorable daughter-in-law, Naomi felt she had to do something, not only to show her deep appreciation, but also to let her know that she wanted her to have a bright future. Therefore she was doing something about it.

Naomi may have done some good thinking and praying, after observing the tenacity of her daughter-in-law's character. I also believe that she did some homework. After all, she was now back home with old friends. She had been away for ten years and things do change, though not as fast as they do these days (2004). She had some friends, trusted friends who brought her up to speed with what was happening. How else would she have known for sure that Boaz would be spending the night alone at the threshing floor, winnowing wheat and barley?

Naomi did some observing, some questioning as well as some listening. She made sure she got her information just right. She had to make sure that the way was clear before she informed Ruth of her plan. She was aware that if she made one wrong move, there could be trouble. She would never do anything that would jeopardize the character or reputation of her beloved daughter-in-law. So she had to make sure that all was clear before giving instructions to Ruth.

There was no indecisiveness after Naomi got her plan together. There was no doubt in her mind. She had no question for Ruth. Her mind was made up. She would let Ruth know that in spite of her grief and bitterness, wisdom was now guiding her every move. She believed that God was about to make a change in both of their lives. Ruth had done all she could to bring comfort to her. Now it was time for her to act on Ruth's behalf.

Therefore in the same courageous manner that Ruth made her pledge, Naomi decided to move ahead with her plan. Nothing was going to get in the way. She was going to let Ruth know that the love and care that she had given her was about to be reciprocated. Naomi's mind was made up and nothing was going to stop her from going ahead with her plan.

RUTH'S OBEDIENCE

When Naomi approached Ruth with her plan to meet Boaz at the threshing floor, she could have asked many questions such as: "Do you think it will be safe for me to go there at night? What if somebody should see me on my way to the farm? How do you think Boaz will feel to see me on his threshing floor? Suppose he has the foreman there with him?" Well, no question was asked. Ruth's confidence in her mother-in-law could not be shaken. She was sure that Naomi would not do anything that would be questionable. Then I think we would not really be charging Ruth wrongfully if we imagine that she had secretly fallen in love with this kind handsome gentleman whom she met on that first day at work.

Ruth was now about to be somewhat subdued. She was not going to talk back to her mother-in-law like she did on the way from Moab. She had made her pledge and that was settled. She had proven to her mother-in-law that she meant what she said by going out in the field with strange folks and worked hard so she could provide for her. Now Naomi was in charge and she was going to be obedient to her. Therefore, when the proposal was presented, Ruth's quick response to Naomi was, "I will do whatever you say."

We can hardly imagine the excitement that Ruth felt as she went searching for her best clothes and her favorite perfume. This was going to be the most exciting experience of her life. She was a little frightened and nervous but was she ever delighted. A few questions crossed her mind again but she knew that Naomi believed her to be a woman of integrity. Therefore, with much joy she prepared herself to do exactly as she was instructed to do. After she was dressed, she showed herself to Naomi and got her approval. With a warm embrace and a great big smile, Naomi wished her God's blessing.

His anger lasts only a moment,
his goodness for a lifetime.
Tears may flow in the night,
but joy comes in the morning.
Psalm 30:5 (TEV)

CHAPTER 11

RUTH GOES TO THE THRESHING FLOOR

Getting to the threshing floor without being noticed was not very easy, but Ruth followed the way Naomi told her to go. She hastened along the path hoping she would meet no one. If she did she would find a way to conceal her identity. She made the journey in record time. She was now at the threshing floor, but could not make her presence known. It was not easy but she would follow her mother-in-law's instruction without fail.

After Boaz had finished his evening meal and rested a while, he decided that work was finished for the day. So he went to lie down at the far end of the pile of grain. He no doubt was protecting his grain from thieves. From her hiding place, Ruth would look to see what Boaz was doing. When she observed that he had fallen asleep, she quietly approached the place where he was, and positioned herself close to his feet as she had been instructed to do. She held her breath for a while hoping he wouldn't hear her breathe. All was quiet. There was not even a mouse anywhere. She listened to the crickets and other night sounds in the distance as the thought to herself, "How did I get to this place? What am I doing here?" She asked herself many questions but got no answer.

In spite of all the excitement, Ruth finally fell asleep. All was quiet until Boaz turned to change position. As he stretched his legs his feet touched something. He was startled. He rubbed his eyes and looked and there was a woman lying at his feet. "Who are you?" he asked: "I am your servant Ruth. Spread the corner of your garment over me, since you are a kinsman redeemer." (Ruth 3:9)

From all appearances, Boaz was delighted to see her there. He spoke kindly to her, as she knew he would. Then he said, "The Lord bless you, my daughter, this kindness is greater than that which you showed earlier: You have not run after younger men, whether rich or poor. And now, my daughter, don't be afraid. I will do for you all you ask. All my fellow townsmen know that you are a woman of noble character." (Ruth 3:10-11) He told her that although he was a kinsman, there was one closer than he, who had the right to redeem her.

He told her to lie down until morning and he would speak to that other kinsman. If he wanted to redeem her, it would be his right to do so. If he refused to redeem her, then as the Lord lives he would do it. So Ruth spent the rest of the night at the feet of Boaz. They were both supposed to be sleeping, but I doubt any of them could. I believe that was the longest night for both of them.

Boaz was planning his speech for the next morning when he would try to meet with the relative that had the first right of redemption. I truly believe that Boaz was praying real hard and hoping that the other kinsman would refuse to redeem Ruth, making the way clear for him to marry the love of his life.

Ruth was lying there trying to sleep also, but how could she? Her mind was working like a grandfather clock that chimed every fifteen minutes and to her it sounded like wedding bells. But what if the kinsman who had the right to redeem her agreed to do so? Would she be able to live with him when Boaz is the one she really loves? Maybe she was thinking, "This is a good time for me to pray to the God under whose wings I have come to take refuge." So, I believe Ruth prayed and Boaz was praying too.

I can't help thinking that Ruth and Boaz were not the only two that spent that sleepless night. I doubt Naomi got any sleep at home. She no doubt spent half the night praying, wishing and hoping. She might have even spent some time pacing the floor, wondering if things went as she planned.

RUTH RETURNS HOME

Early in the morning while it was still dark Boaz spoke to Ruth saying, "Don't let it be known that a woman came to the threshing floor." He was protecting his good name but more so that of his beloved

Ruth. Too much was at stake. Boaz was such a gentleman. He was caring for Ruth as he would for his daughter. He loved and respected her too much to expose her to gossip. Before sending her on her way, he said, "Bring me the shawl you are wearing and hold it out." When she did so, he poured into it six measures of barley and put it on her. Then he went back to town.

One can scarcely imagine what was going on in Ruth's mind and heart as she hurried home from the threshing floor. She was moving very fast for two reasons: She wanted to get home before anyone could see her. Can you imagine the news around town that day if someone had seen her leaving Boaz's threshing floor? I don't believe that people were that much different than they are today. In every age there are men of integrity who can be trusted even when they find themselves in tight spots. At such times they do not depend on their own strength but rather on that which God gives to those who call on Him.

Another reason Ruth was in a big hurry, she could hardly wait to get home to share the experience with her friend and mother Naomi. She was the one who made the plan to begin with. As she hurried along, she kept hoping she would meet no one on the way. She might have prayed as she started and believed that God who had already done such incredible things for her, would hear and answer her prayers and He did.

I doubt Ruth had ever walked at that speed before. Along with the two reasons she had for getting home fast, she had a private reason that she held close to her heart. She was in love with a wonderful man who had promised to marry her, if by any means he could. As she traveled in the darkness, the light of love was all over her. She could scarcely believe what was happening to her. It was somewhat of a Cinderella story. She must have stopped for a minute, pinched her arm and ask, "Is this for real, or am I dreaming and walking in my sleep?"

Ruth was assured she was not dreaming neither was she walking in her sleep. As she proceeded along a narrow, rocky path, she slipped and almost fell. She caught herself and felt as though the hand of her beloved Boaz had held her close. The branches overhanging the path brushed against her face, leaving the cold drops of morning dew on her cheeks which felt like a gentle kiss that would last forever. She took a deep breath of the fresh morning air and felt as though she could win any race.

Ruth continued walking briskly. She couldn't stop thinking of the exciting night she had spent at Boaz's threshing floor. She thought of the kind way he treated her. He was such a gentle person, yet had such strength of character. She treasured every kind word he said to her and kept repeating them as she went along. She recalled how careful he was as he placed the bundle of barley on her head. She also recalled the gentle touch of his hand on her shoulder and said, "Take good care my daughter."

Ruth made the journey home in record time. When she got to the house it was still dark. She unloaded the bundle of barley on the step and decided to be quiet with her thoughts before going inside. Hugging herself, she smiled and leaned on the bundle of barley as if leaning on Boaz. She was so happy she bowed her head and whispered a prayer of thanks to her new found God. She sat very still for a while, reflecting and enjoying every moment of her reflections. She smiled and thought, "It is so wonderful to love and be loved." She was very thoughtful about her mother-in-law and if she was asleep, she didn't want to disturb her rest. So she sat and waited until the darkness began to disappear then she opened the door.

NAOMI WAS WAITING

Although Ruth was extremely careful in entering the house, she was surprised to hear Naomi's voice saying, "Is that you my daughter?" Ruth quickly responded, "Yes mother, it is I." Naomi quickly joined her. She was anxious to know if Ruth had followed the plan as she had instructed and to know what happened.

Ruth was unloading the bundle of barley when her mother-in-law walked in. Ruth embraced her and said good morning. Before she could say anything more, Naomi quickly asked, "How did it go my daughter?" Ruth was delighted to share the good news with her. So she told her every detail of what took place on the threshing floor and that she followed all the instructions exactly as she told her.

Ruth joyfully expressed herself to her mother-in-law. Then she told her, "He gave me these six measures of barley, saying, "Don't go back to your mother-in-law empty handed." This gift was a gesture of good will and assurance to Naomi. Boaz was really saying to her, "I care about your future. I care about your daughter-in-law also. The truth is, I'm in love with her and if I can redeem her I will." Naomi understood better than any other person could. So she gladly accepted the gift that was sent to her.

TIME TO WAIT

At this time Naomi felt that her plan to secure a good future for her daughter-in-law was beginning to show signs of progress. She had great hope that the God she served was about to answer her prayer. She felt a sense of peace. She felt good about what was happening.

Ruth was overwhelmed with great expectation. She was having a time of great celebration. She walked around with quick steps. There was a sparkle in her eyes. One look at her and you could tell she was one happy camper. She no doubt began to suggest making plans for her wedding. Naomi was happy for her too and was pleased to see such a change in her conduct. But wisdom told her that it was time to say a few sobering words to her elated daughter-in-law.

Naomi did not want to put a damper on her daughter-in-law's spirit. The plan so far seemed to be going well. She did not doubt that God was at work in their lives and would finish what He had started. She also knew that there was the possibility that things could change. She could not be sure that what they were hoping for would happen just as they thought. She did not want to see Ruth build up her hope in one direction and be disappointed if things did not go the way she thought they would. So she gave her a motherly advice which went like this:

> "Wait, my daughter, until you find out what happens. For the man will not rest until the matter is settled today."
>
> (Ruth 3: 18)

Waiting is not always easy, especially when we are anxious about something.

But it's a lesson that each of us have to learn at one time or another. Ruth had discovered that the God she was learning to trust does hear and answer prayers. She was observing his power at work in her life as well as that of her mother-in-law. She also needed to know that God does not give us everything we ask for at the time when we want it. So her mother-in-law said, "Wait my daughter."

There is a waiting period for most things. One must learn that waiting does not mean denial. In the natural, we sow seeds but must wait for them to grow and develop. In the physical, a surgeon will perform surgery but there is a waiting period for healing. In the spiritual, we must also wait for God's plan to unfold. We cannot hurry God. My mother who passed away many years ago, had a favorite verse of scripture that she would quote in most of her letters to me: "Wait on the Lord; Be of good courage, and He shall strengthen your heart; Wait I say on the Lord." (Psalm 27:14) It seems to be something that mothers feel they ought to say to their daughters. Don't be in a rush to get into a relationship. Waiting for a while is wisdom.

His anger lasts only a moment,
his goodness for a lifetime.
Tears may flow in the night,
but joy comes in the morning.
Psalm 30:5 (TEV)

CHAPTER 12

BOAZ: A NOBLEMAN

While Naomi and Ruth were having their conversations at home, Boaz was on his way to work on the business at hand. He knew that he was not the first in line to be the kinsman-redeemer. There was another person ahead of him. He also knew that something had to be done for Naomi and Ruth. He was a caring, sensitive man. He had the wellbeing of these two women at heart. Yes, he loved Ruth with all his heart and wished that he could make her his wife, but he was going to go about it the right way. From all appearances, Boaz was an outstanding citizen of his community. The way he greeted his workers on his farm and their respectful response to him spoke volumes. When he discovered Ruth gleaning in his field as a stranger, he extended to her both hospitality and protection. He told the young men working in the field not to touch her.

Boaz did not only commend Ruth for the care and love she had shown to her mother-in-law. He complimented her on the choice she had made to put her trust in God. He had asked God's blessing on her as she worked in the field. He was not aware that God was using him to bring back joy and happiness to these two women.

Boaz had been thinking kindly of Ruth all along. But he knew that if he followed the laws and customs of his time he would not be the one to redeem her. Moreover, from his response to her at the threshing floor, he thought she would have been interested in a younger man. Therefore, when Ruth proposed to him by reminding him that he was a kinsman-redeemer, he blessed her and told her that requesting him to marry her represented a greater kindness than that shown to her mother-in-law at the beginning.

Even though the request from Ruth to marry her was one Boaz did not expect, he promised her that he would do things the right way. There was another kinsman who was first in line. He needed to find out if he was willing to be her redeemer. If he was unable or if he refused to fulfill his duty, then Boaz was next in line and would by all means carry out his duty to her. Therefore, after he hurried to the town gate he sat and waited.

Boaz knew that the one who had first choice to be kinsman-redeemer, would be coming by. As soon as he saw him, he called to him and asked him to take a seat. Boaz was an astute businessman, and he wanted to do things right. So he called ten of the Elders of the city and asked them to share in the discussion. Without delay, Boaz presented his case by saying:

"Naomi who has come back from Moab, is selling the piece of land that belonged to our brother Elimelech. I thought I should bring the matter to your attention and suggest that you buy it in the presence of these seated here and in the presence of the Elders of my people. If you will redeem it, do so. But if you will not, tell me, so I will know. For no one has the right to do it except you, and I am next in line."

(Ruth 4: 3-4)

Right away without hesitation, the kinsman-redeemer agreed to purchase the property. I think Boaz, the shrewd businessman, may have whispered to himself, "Hold it there my brother, not so fast. It is not over yet." Then Boaz reminded him that according to the law, if he bought the property, he would also have to marry Elimelech's son, Mahlon's wife, Ruth. Now on second thought the kinsman changed his mind. One commentator suggests that the kinsman did not want to complicate his inheritance. He might have feared that if he had a son by Ruth, some of his estate would transfer away from his family to the family of Elimelech. Whatever his reason, the way was now clear for Boaz to marry Ruth.

This was a decisive moment for Boaz. He did not ask the kinsman to go home and discuss it with his family. He did not tell him to go home and think it over. He was too clever a businessman to allow a good bargain to slip away from him. He had made a promise to Ruth and he was going to be true to his word.

The transfer of property at that time was quite simple, but meaningful and binding. One party would remove his sandal and give it to the other. This was how transactions were legalized in Israel. The kinsman-redeemer told Boaz to buy the property. Then he removed his sandal. Right away Boaz called on the Elders to bear witness that he was purchasing from Naomi, all the property of Elimelech, Kilion and Mahlon. Then he went on to inform them, "I have also acquired Ruth the Moabitess, Mahlon's widow as my wife, in order to maintain the name of the dead with his property, so that his name will not disappear from among his family or from the town records. Today you are witnesses!" All the Elders responded in the affirmative. Then they pronounced a blessing on him and the wife that he was about to marry.

Naomi knew that Boaz was a man of honesty and integrity. If she hadn't, she would never have trusted to send her beloved daughter-in-law to his threshing floor when he was there alone that night. She also knew that he was a man who kept his promise. He could be trusted to do what he said he would do. That is why she had confidently said to Ruth, "Wait my daughter, until you find out what happens. For the man will not rest until the matter is settled today." Naomi was right, and we applaud Boaz for these enviable and admirable qualities. He must have been a wonderful example and mentor to the young men of his day.

This most charming and beautiful romantic story continues. It tells us that Boaz took Ruth and she became his wife. But I can't help wishing that we could know exactly what Boaz did after he knew he was free to marry Ruth. If he had lived in the twenty first century, there is no doubt that he would have a cell phone. He would have found a quiet place to make a call. This is what he might have said, "Ruth, my darling, I can hardly wait to see you. I have just left the town gate where I met with the kinsman-redeemer and the Elders. The kinsman has decided that he is not able to perform the duty as a redeemer. So, guess what? I am free to marry you my dear."

Boaz might have continued with his exciting news, "Ruth my beloved, please tell your mother-in-law the wonderful news. I know she will be happy for you. Tell her that I am on my way home to take a shower and change my work clothes. I will be over to see you as soon as I can. Oh Ruth. How can I be so blessed of the Lord? Imagine you and I being able to get married and spend the rest of our lives together. I'm so happy, I can't wait to see you. I know you are happy too."

On the other end, Ruth no doubt would be so overjoyed, she might be speechless. Then again, she might have let out a scream and run to her mother-in-law. "Mother, Boaz just called. He said he met with the kinsman-redeemer at the town gate with the Elders. The kinsman is not able to perform his duty. Therefore Boaz is free to do it and he says he is going to marry me."

Well, there were no cell phones but I know that someway, somehow, the news was communicated and it was joyful news. I also think that Naomi and Ruth hugged each other and might have even shed some tears of joy mingled with gratitude and praise to God. They might have even danced around the floor, giving thanks to God for having brought them to this moment. Naomi who had been overcome with grief and bitterness could see the hand of a loving God reaching out to her in a new way. Ruth had walked in disguise and darkness from the threshing floor. Now she was basking in the light of a new beginning. She could scarcely believe what was taking place in her once hopeless life. I can see her on her knees beside her bed in a private prayer of thanks to the God under whose wings she had come to take refuge.

His anger lasts only a moment,
his goodness for a lifetime.
Tears may flow in the night,
but joy comes in the morning.
Psalm 30:5 (TEV)

CHAPTER 13

TIME FOR A WEDDING

We are not sure how long it might have taken Boaz to go to see Ruth and Naomi. They might have had a nice meal prepared for him by the time he got to their place. Since Ruth was instructed by her mother-in-law to put on her best clothes and perfume herself when she was going to the threshing floor, we can imagine that she had to do something similar when Boaz was coming to see her. This would really be their first date. Naomi decided to fix the meal while Ruth straightened up the house and got ready for the great occasion. Ruth could hardly contain herself. She quickly recalled that first morning when she walked out the door of their house to find a field to glean in. She had no idea where she was going. She recalled meeting Boaz in the field for the first time. She had been so surprised and honored that he took notice of her that she bowed down to the ground in gratitude. Now here she was, dressed and waiting to fall in his arms to greet him as her future husband.

We can only imagine the time of fellowship that was shared by these three very special people. Naomi's match making plan had worked. She had accomplished her heart's desire for her very special daughter-in-law. She did not have to be concerned about her as she was before. She was pleased that Ruth would never have to go to anybody's field to glean again. She also knew that between Boaz and Ruth, her own needs would be met. Ruth felt very thankful to her mother-in-law for the interest that she took in her. Her threshing floor experience was one she would never forget. The moments of fellowship and joy they shared together would never be forgotten either. Boaz was overwhelmed with gratitude to Naomi for the motherly advice she had given to her daughter-in-law. How could he ever repay her? He took time to express his thanks to her. It might have been a long time since he had such a special meal prepared for him. So he expressed his appreciation to Naomi for preparing it. Then he looked at his beloved Ruth with such kind eyes and thanked her for choosing him. Ruth's cheeks became rosy as she blushed at his tenderness toward her. It was a special time for all three as they shared their gratitude to God for bringing them together.

We wish that something had been recorded about the plans for the wedding. We can imagine that as Ruth, Naomi and Boaz met together, they discussed plans for the wedding. There seemed to be no reason to wait. So they must have started right away to make the arrangements. Weddings have always been an exciting time. Special preparations and much planning is the order of the day. It is an emotional time, not only for the bride and groom, but also for family and friends. It is a time of celebration and happiness.

So although nothing is recorded about the wedding of Ruth and Boaz, we can imagine that there was much cause for celebration. Boaz was a wealthy man and a generous person also. There had to be a wedding feast. I think Naomi and her women friends got together with Ruth and did some good planning. I also believe that whatever the cost, Boaz was more than happy to take care of it.

Whatever the circumstances were, Boaz and Ruth were married. All that has been said about the marriage is, "Boaz took Ruth and she became his wife." After the marriage, Ruth became pregnant and gave birth to a son. We are not certain how long Ruth had been married to her first husband before he died. We know that she had no children with him. Now she is married to her second husband and gives birth to a baby boy.

NAOMI: A GRANDMOTHER

Ruth's determination was to stand by her mother-in-law no matter what the cost. Ruth's thoughtfulness was talked about and admired by the people of the town. Her kindness remained unchanged. Naomi on the other hand, did not decide to sit and allow Ruth to work and take care of her. She made every effort to reciprocate. She knew that Ruth was young and beautiful. She was caring and unselfish. She was industrious and would be a good wife to another man as she had been to her son. Naomi wanted to help in bringing some support, some stability and joy to her widowed daughter-in-law. So she planned, encouraged, supported and assisted Ruth in every way she could. Her unselfishness now becomes her blessing.

This baby boy was a joy to Ruth and her husband. He was their first child. Boaz was delighted that the beautiful young woman he met on his farm that day had not only become his beloved wife, she was now the mother of his child. There was much happiness in that household.

Although Ruth was the mother and Boaz the father of this child, Naomi took center stage. The town's women were happy that Ruth became a mother. But as they looked at the Naomi whom they had known before she went away to Moab, as a happy, pleasant person and who had returned sad and bitter, they rejoiced. She was not only looking like the person she used to be, she was now a new person. She was renewed, refreshed and happy. Her women friends rejoiced with her by saying:

"Praise be to the Lord, who this day has not left you without a kinsman-redeemer. May he become famous throughout Israel! He will renew your life and sustain you in your old age. For your daughter-in-law, who is better to you than seven sons, has given him birth. Then Naomi took the child, laid him in her lap and cared for him. The women living there said, "Naomi has a son." And they named him Obed. He was the father of Jesse, the father of David."

(Ruth 4:14-17)

The women believed that God had done a good thing for Ruth. She was deserving of a good, honest, respectable, thoughtful and wealthy man. From their action, they believed that Ruth could be blessed with other children. But as far as they were concerned, this baby belonged to Naomi. The joy that these women were expressing was not just because Naomi had become a grandmother. It was a special experience, because Naomi did not only have a grandchild, which was wonderful, but this baby was conceived with Naomi in mind by the daughter-in-law who loved her and as the women said, "Was better to her than seven sons." The birth of a son was considered to be a great blessing. So, for the women to say that Ruth was better to Naomi than seven sons was an outstanding complement.

His anger lasts only a moment,
his goodness for a lifetime.
Tears may flow in the night,
but joy comes in the morning.
Psalm 30:5 (TEV)

CHAPTER 14

RUTH'S REWARD

When Ruth decided to accompany Naomi, her beloved mother-in-law back to her home in Bethlehem, she had no idea what the outcome would be. Ruth's desire and determination was to stay close to her, share her pain, comfort her and find a way to support her so she could be cared for the rest of her life. God had a great reward for Ruth even though she was not aware of it at the start.

According to Dr Herbert Lockyer, Ruth deserved the fullest reward for her decision to serve God and her unselfish devotion to a widowed mother-in-law. How delicate and tender was that midnight meeting in the threshing floor! Discovering Ruth there, Boaz recognized the fear her womanly reserve prompted. Thoughts of purity and goodness alone passed between them. The, "Fear not" and "My daughter" constituted the tribute of Boaz to Ruth's virtue, and revealed his own nobility and character."(All The Books And Chapters Of The Bible).

Ruth made the right choice in deciding to stay

with her mother-in-law. It was not an easy choice to make. It meant leaving family, friends and country to go with Naomi who was overcome with grief and did not know what to make of it all. The God that Ruth decided to claim as her own and trust to care for her granted her more than she had hoped for. There was great joy in her heart as she watched Naomi taking care of little Obed. She wished that her family in Moab could see her now. She had a respectable, gentle, honest and wealthy husband. Her baby was beautiful and a joy to all.

GOD'S PROVIDENTIAL CARE

God is sovereign, and is at work in the lives of those who put their trust in Him. He is a God of surprises. He does not need to be instructed by anyone. He chooses whom he will in order to work his purpose out. For God to have brought a Moabite widow to be united in marriage with a respected Israelite leader at the time he did was very unlikely. On that first day when Ruth said to her mother-in-law, "Let me go to the fields and pick up the left over grain behind anyone in whose eyes I find favor," it seemed as though she was taking a blind leap into the unknown.

Having heard that there was a law that permitted poor people to go in the fields and pick up what fell from the reapers, Ruth decided to take a chance. She was willing to go to any field that was available. I do believe that she prayed and asked the God she had learned about and accepted in her life, to direct her as she ventured out. We can also imagine that her beloved mother-in-law also offered a prayer for her.

Therefore, although it seemed as if Ruth entered the field of Boaz, who happened to be a kinsman-redeemer purely by accident, it wasn't. It was all a part of God's providence at work. Yes, Ruth was from a country whose people were not considered friends to the people she was now living with. She even considered herself inferior to the servant girls that worked in the field for Boaz. But the amazing grace of God, looked beyond what others, including herself, thought and saw her worth and her need.

God chooses unlikely people through whom He works to carry out his plan. Ruth was indeed one of those people. It has been said that Moabites represented temptation and trouble for Israel. (Exodus 15: 15; Num. 25:1; Jud. 3: 12-30) That fact of history did not prevent God from using a dedicated Moabite woman to carry out his saving purpose for the world. God works with people from all nations and races to accomplish His will in ways that often surprise us. Ruth was not only the great grandmother of David, who was the least of his brothers to be chosen as king. Boaz, Ruth, their son Obed, their grandson Jesse and their great-grandson, David, are named in the genealogy of Jesus our Savior, in the first chapter of the book of Matthew.

His anger lasts only a moment,
his goodness for a lifetime.
Tears may flow in the night,
but joy comes in the morning.
Psalm 30:5 (TEV)

CHAPTER 15

NAOMI- RUTH-BOAZ: WHAT CAN WE LEARN FROM THEM?

NAOMI:

The life experiences of Naomi, reminds us that loss and grief are part of the human existence. We observe also that in the throws of loss and grief, it is a normal reaction to be sad, angry, bitter and overwhelmed. When a wife loses a spouse, it has to be difficult, especially if they cared a lot for each other. I have talked with widows, and they tell me that they do not just suffer the loss of their mate. One told a group of us wives, that when her husband passed away some people treated her so different that she couldn't understand. Another widow told me that friends who associated with her and her husband, became distant when he died. She said, "It was as though I had a disease that they didn't want to catch." It was much worse being a widow at the time Naomi lost her husband.

The pain of losing a spouse does not go away any time soon. A short time after Naomi lost her husband she also lost both of her sons. She had a good husband who cared for his family. His reason for relocating to Moab was to better provide for them. Now he was gone and her two sons also. This was more grief than Naomi thought she could endure.

My husband and I lost our son, Patrick. As his mother, I feel as if a part of my body is out there somewhere. The grief and pain cannot be put into words. After almost three years the intense grief has subsided, but the absence of his person does not leave our minds. We watched him graduate from grade school, high school and college. We saw him achieve many of his dreams. He called home every weekend and any other time he felt like it. He came to visit as often as he could and loved to come home. He loved and enjoyed his nuclear as well as his extended family. We don't expect him to come home any more. His favorite and only seven year old nephew Kaelon has to be comforted quite often because he can't play games with uncle Pat any more. We are a large family and he is missed by all. He had many friends and they continue to miss him.

I really wonder how Naomi felt in a strange country with all this grief. Yet, we learn from her that it's OK to grieve, be sad, and even be angry. It's OK if we feel that we have to blame someone. If we can't find anybody to blame, we can blame God like she did. God can take it. He knows what he is doing and he also understands that we do not have a clue as to what His overall plans are. He is full of compassion. "For the Lord will not cast off for ever. But though He cause grief, yet will He have compassion according to the multitude of His mercies. For He does not afflict willingly nor grieve the children of men," (Lamentations 3: 31-33). We learn also that God does not take away trials from our lives. He gives us enduring grace and although weeping may endure for a night, joy will come in the morning.

NAOMI: THE MODEL MOTHER-IN-LAW

In today's society, when someone says, "Let me tell you about my mother-in-law, we expect some kind of negative statement or humorous anecdote, because the mother-in-law caricature has been a standard centerpiece of ridicule or comedy. The book of Ruth however, tells a different story." (Life Application Bible) The relationship between Naomi and Ruth is a beautiful example of how mothers-in-law and daughters-in –law should live.

Mothers around the world are respected for who they are. Mothers are special in every culture. I remember when I was in grade school, nothing could get a child into a fight any faster than when one says something about his or her mother. When I hear the negative remarks that some people make about mothers-in-law, I often wonder, what are the changes that take place between being a mother and becoming a mother-in-law?

As I loaded my groceries on the check out counter at a Publix supermarket, I observed a very nervous woman ahead of me. "Hurry up please, I don't want my daughter-in-law to come before I get through the line." "Where is your daughter-in-law?" I asked as the lady kept her head up high, looking in all directions.

"She is somewhere in the store, but I have to get out of this line before she comes or I will get an ear full. All that daughters-in-law want is what is in your purse. After that they have no use for you." She hurriedly paid for the things she had then went and stood to wait for her daughter-in-law. She seemed so upset and unhappy. I hoped that they would not have to live in the same house.

The clerk who waited on the lady whispered to me, "That is so sad." I turned to the lady next in line behind me and asked if she had a daughter-in-law. "Oh yes!" she said with a big smile, "I have a wonderful daughter-in-law. We love each other and we get along just fine. I don't know what I'd do without her." I've heard many comedians tell negative jokes about mothers-in-law. In real life though, I have heard of more good relationships between daughters-in-law and their mothers-in-law than negative ones. Naomi has set a good example for women as she models her involvement with Ruth.

TRAGEDY AND TRIALS

From the time we are born into this world, we become prime candidates for pain and sorrow. We read in the Holy Scriptures that, "Man born of woman is of few days and full of trouble." (Job 14:1) One does not have to go looking for trouble. It will find us at one time or another. Sometimes young people are looked upon as carefree and think only of having fun. Well, those of us who have not forgotten that we were young once upon a long time, don't think so.

Young people ought to be happy and enjoy some fun. There are enough serious times awaiting them further along in life. Youth is a wonderful time to dream and set goals. It is also a time when they face many challenges including trials and tragedy. Troubles, trials and tragedies do not discriminate. There is no respect for one age above another. Trouble can come to the young, the old, and those in between, but the hurt is the same. Tragedy has a way of making us feel as if we are pushed into a dark corner with no way out. Sometimes there are those who have trusted God for years. Then in a time of tragedy they feel like asking, "Where is God my maker, who giveth songs in the night?" (Job 35:10)

Some time ago a friend of mine was going through a devastating experience. I could empathize because, not only had I gone through some trying times, but I was sharing her grief. She is one who has trusted God in the past and knows what He has done and is still able to do. Yet, at this time when I reminded her of God's unfailing love and care, she said, "You know what, sometimes I wonder if God is anywhere around."

I did not push my encouragement any further or try to convince her. I felt her pain and tried to understand. I knew that she could not see the hand of God at the moment. Her eyes were dimmed with grief.

Still I had the assurance that she knew that her heavenly Father would not allow despondency to overwhelm her.

Like Naomi, we sometimes feel as if the hand of God is gone out against us. Somewhere in our mind there is this question, "If God loves and cares about me, why is this happening to me? Why am I being punished?" We try to find answers but they are nowhere to be found. Naomi told Ruth to wait and see how things would work out. So she did and God took care of her. We too must wade through our trials and grief until the change comes. Maybe you've heard these words before, "God may not come when you want Him to, but He will always be on time."

I had just finished writing this paragraph and went in my kitchen for lunch. When I was through eating, I picked up Charles Swindoll's book, "Hope Again." My sister, Amy, sent me that book as a gift when our son was taken away so suddenly. I had read it before, but I believe that no good book should be read once and then put away. I sat and read a few pages before resuming my writing. I came across these words which I share with you:

"Suffering is a universal language. Tears are the same for Jews or Muslims or Christians, for white or black or brown, for children or adults or elderly. When life hurts and dreams fade, we may express our anguish in different ways, but each one of us knows the sting of pain and heartache, disease and disaster, trials and sufferings. Joseph Parker a great preacher of yesteryear, once said to a group of aspiring ministers, 'Preach to the suffering and you will never lack a congregation. There is a broken heart in every pew.'"

I believe that this beautiful planet on which we live would be even more beautiful if we gave more attention to these facts. Yes, broken hearts and lonely lives are all around us. Naomi's suffering of long ago, is as relevant as today's suffering that is a part of each of our lives. We need to be aware also, that because everyone has a time of trial in his or her life, does not make our hurt any less. Therefore we need a strong arm on which to lean when troubles come our way. We can remember that, "The eyes of the Lord are upon the righteous and His ears are open unto their cry." (Psalm 34:15)

Even though sometimes we feel as if we have had more than our share of trials, if we look around us and ask a few questions, we will find that there are still those who have had more tough times than we have. In some of my troubled times, I find myself singing this song written by Elisha Hoffman:

I must tell Jesus all of my trials
I cannot bear these burdens alone;
In my distress He kindly will help me
He always loves and cares for his own.

I must tell Jesus all of my troubles;
He is a kind compassionate friend
If I but ask Him He will deliver
Make of my troubles quickly an end.

Tempted and tried I need a great Savior,

One who can help my burdens to bear
I must tell Jesus, I must tell Jesus;
He all my cares and sorrows will share.

In times of trouble and trial, we need strength beyond our human capability. Therefore, we must go to the source of abundance, which is God alone. Naomi recognized the hand of God in her life and gave thanks to Him. She was still a widow. She was still missing her sons but her bitterness was gone by the grace of God. The women in the community also recognized the hand of God and His great compassion. So they expressed their thanks and shared her joy.

We learn also that Naomi was not only a model mother-in-law. She was also a good friend. Not only was this true in her relationship with Ruth, she was a friend of those women who rejoiced with her and pronounced a blessing on her. We are admonished in the word of God to, "Rejoice with them that do rejoice, and weep with them that weep. (Romans 12:15) We do so because we never know when our time of trouble or joy will come. Naomi has set a good example for us as we observe her relationship with her daughters-in-law. Her life models this verse found in Psalms:

Happy are those who are strong in the Lord
Who set their minds on a pilgrimage to
    Jerusalem.
When they walk through the valley of
    weeping,

It will become a place of refreshing springs,
Where pools of blessing collect after the
    rain!
They will continue to grow stronger,
And each of them will appear before God in
    Jerusalem.

(Psalm 84: 5-7 NLT)

His anger lasts only a moment,
his goodness for a lifetime.
Tears may flow in the night,
but joy comes in the morning.
Psalm 30:5 (TEV)

CHAPTER 16

RUTH: THE MODEL DAUGHTER-IN-LAW

"Ruth's fervent speech to her mother-in-law Naomi, is one of the most beautiful declarations of authentic family love in the Bible. Even though not addressed to husband wife relationship, it is often used in wedding ceremonies to describe what marital love should be. It affirms the desire to be together, to face life's challenges together, to be a family, and worship the same God. All of these elements are central to a healthy Christian marriage when Christ becomes the Lord who makes the Father's presence known to the family" (Disciple's Study Bible)

If we agree that Naomi is a model mother-in-law, then Ruth can be called a model daughter-in-law. She has shown us the capacity of the human heart for love. We learn from her how God rewards a life of faith, humility, devotion and determination. We also learn that God can use whomever he chooses. He will use anyone who is willing to be used by Him. We also learn that God has placed limitless potential in the human spirit. She shows us that when we are challenged, if we believe and trust in God, He will enable us to rise to our potential and grow into the person we are created to become.

Ruth left her gods in Moab and embraced the true God that her mother-in-law worshiped. That was the greatest decision she ever made. Life took on new meaning for her and she was never the same. Those of us who have made the choice of accepting God as the object of our love, devotion and worship, can attest to the change that has taken place in our lives. Worshiping God does not make us immune to trouble, but we are assured that He will be with us as we face our difficulties.

MIRACLES DO HAPPEN

When Ruth promised Naomi that she was never going to leave her, she meant every word. That same kind of determination that she displayed in her speech to her on their journey back to Bethlehem, is a God given trait in all of us. We can make up our minds to do what seems impossible. With the help of God we can do whatever we dream of doing, because nothing is impossible with God. Every person, who reads the story of Ruth can emulate her determination, her courage, her diligence and her humble spirit.

Ruth decided to provide food for her mother-in-law. When she learned that there was a way for her to work for it, she jumped at the first opportunity. She did not wait to see if there would be an easier way. If the price to be paid was bending in the hot sun all day, she was ready. If she was going to be looked at as being poor and destitute, she was not going to think about it. She was going to do what ever it took.

My father was a carpenter and a furniture maker. He worked very hard, but sometimes the people he worked for would pay only a part of the money that was due. He had men who worked for him, so he had to pay them. Many times there was little left after he paid his workers. With a family of ten children to feed and clothe, it was very difficult. As a child listening to him talk with my mother, I would feel badly when I knew how hard he worked. Then one day during one of these discussions, I heard my dad say, "I don't care what happens. No child of mine is ever going to go to bed hungry." We never did.

My husband lives by the same philosophy. There was no honest job that he would not do to support his family. There is no sacrifice he would not make for the well being of his children. He has always felt that's what being a father is all about.

Like Ruth we can decide to do what is right to do and do it. Ruth is a good example of what a friend should be. We all need a friend like her and since we need a friend, we should be one. I don't have a best friend. I think that a friend should not have to be enhanced by an adjective. There is no bad friend. If someone is not what a friend should be you don't need to call them one. Ralph Waldo Emerson put friendship in these words: "The glory of friendship is not so much in the out-stretched hand or even the kindly smile. It is in the spiritual inspiration that comes when you discover that someone else believes in you and is willing to trust you with his friendship."

A friend is one on whom you can depend. A friend can be trusted always. A friend loves at all times. In the book of Proverbs we read: "There is a friend that sticks closer than a brother." (Proverbs 18:24) Ruth was a friend like that and she reminds us of what we can become when we make the right choice.

KINDNESS IN GRIEF

Another lesson we can learn from the story of Ruth, is how to be patient and kind to those who are grieving. Grief will cause you to do what others cannot understand, and they really don't need to. About a year after our family had experienced the sudden loss of two family members, my sister and I were in a beauty shop. While sitting there, we listened to three women having some real good laughs at someone they knew who was grieving the loss of a child. They laughed about how many times this mother goes to the cemetery with flowers. They thought that was so stupid when the child was already dead.

As I listened to the conversation of those women, they sounded so cold toward a person who was grieving so deeply. Having gone through my own experience, I could understand that the lady was trying to cope with her loss the best she could. I asked the women a few questions about the grieving person. Then I suggested to them that she was only trying to help herself through her grief. When my sister told them that we both were grieving for the two unexpected deaths in our family they were a little less vocal. We soon discovered that none of them had ever lost a friend or close relative. Knowing what I was feeling even then, I recalled the words of William Shakespeare: "Everyone can master a grief but he that has it." He lived 1564-1616 but people are the same even today in the year 2004. "The Lord is close to the broken hearted and saves those who are crushed in spirit. A righteous man may have many troubles; but the Lord delivers him from them all." (Psalm 34: 18-19)

We learn that God is ever present in the lives of those who put their trust in Him. He is present in tragedies, in grief, in suffering, in frustrations, in bitterness, in crisis, in difficulties and in our pain. In our darkest moments, He is in the shadow and we can trust Him. It is then that we walk by faith and not by sight. His grace will be sufficient to take us through all our difficulties. Through these trying times, He is working to perfect the persons he meant for us to be.

Like Ruth, there are hidden qualities in each of us that only God sees. This poem describes not only the life of Ruth, but also yours and mine.

> In the bulb there is a flower
> In the seed, an apple tree
> In cocoon, a hidden promise
> Butterflies will soon be free!

In the cold and snow of winter,
There's a spring that waits to be,
Unrevealed until the season,
Something God alone can see.

There's a song in every silence,
Seeking word and melody,
There's a dawn in every darkness,
Bringing hope to you and me.

From the past will come the future,
What it holds is a mystery,
Unrevealed until the season,
Something God alone can see.

In our end is our beginning,
In our time infinity,
In our doubt, there is believing,
In our life, eternity.

In our death a resurrection,
At the last a victory,
Unrevealed until its season,
Something God alone can see.

Author Unknown

His anger lasts only a moment,
his goodness for a lifetime.
Tears may flow in the night,
but joy comes in the morning.
Psalm 30:5 (TEV)

CHAPTER 17

BOAZ: THE GENTLEMAN

B oaz was not only a gentleman, he was a gentle man. He respected his employees and they respected him. One only has to listen to the exchange of greetings between them to know that this was true. He blessed them and they blessed him in return. Employers who treat their employees with respect and kindness, get respect and good service in return. Boaz could be considered a model boss. He took God into his business and he was blessed. He did not only care for his workers, he paid attention to those who were gleaning on his farm: the widow, the poor and the alien.

When he inquired and discovered who Ruth was, he went and talked with her and made her feel welcome on his farm. He treated her with respect. He was the kind of boss that had lunch with his workers and he invited Ruth to have lunch with them. He even gave her some of what had been prepared for him. He was so generous with the meal. After Ruth ate and was satisfied she had enough left over to take home to her grieving mother-in-law. I do believe that Boaz had that in mind as he shared his meal with Ruth.

Boaz offered protection to Ruth. He knew that this strange, beautiful young woman could be a temptation to those men working in the field, especially if they thought she was poor. So he called his men together and ordered them not to touch her. He had keen foresight and did not wait for something to happen. He made sure it didn't. He was a kind, considerate man. He knew that Ruth had suffered much grief along with Naomi. He knew she had traveled a long way from Moab to Bethlehem. He understood that she was selflessly in the field to gather food for her beloved mother-in-law. So he told his reapers to purposely drop some barley, so she wouldn't have to work so hard. What a guy! What a gentleman! Ruth left his field that day feeling like a new and blessed person and indeed she was.

BOAZ AT THE THRESHING FLOOR

Boaz, a single man could have taken advantage of Ruth that night at the threshing floor. But he was too honorable a man to stoop to that. His first words when he discovered that the woman at his feet was Ruth were, "The Lord bless you my daughter." He acknowledged God in their company. Then he told her not to be afraid. He treated her like a kind father would his daughter.

Boaz was a man of his word. He was a man who kept his promise. He could be depended on. He was unselfish. He was thoughtful, he was honest and a man of impeccable character. He was the kind of person any woman would desire to have as a life time companion. He was wealthy and blessed of God. He was a super guy.

GOD WORKS THROUGH BOAZ

We haven't a clue as to how God thinks and how he plans to work His divine purpose out in the lives of His created beings. Here was Boaz a wealthy bachelor and businessman, overseeing his farm. He was managing his affairs and prospering. He was not only a good businessman. The most outstanding quality about him was that he was a man that feared God. He seemed quite content with the life he was leading.

Some ladies may have looked at Boaz, the eligible bachelor and wondered if he would ever get married. I imagine that there were some very fine women in the community who might have been pleased if Boaz had asked them to marry him. That was not to be. God had already selected the woman he wanted Boaz to marry. Even though the people of Moab were thought of as unfriendly to the people of Judah, God in His infinite wisdom brought these two wonderful people together. Boaz seemed to have been preoccupied with his service to Jehovah, treating his employees the way he thought they should be treated and living a life of honor and integrity. Showing kindness to others was his way of life.

God was keeping record of all he did and planning to give him a full reward. At the same time Ruth was also preoccupied with forgetting her own discomfort and showering kindness to her grief stricken mother-in-law. God was paying attention to her also. Therefore, although it seemed as if Ruth had just stumbled on to the field of Boaz, it was not so. God had dispatched an angel that guided her feet in the path that led her there. Therefore, as they encountered each other on that first day in the field, it was love at first sight.

God does not need instruction from anyone in order to work his plan. His eyes are all over his creation. Geography is no barrier to Him. Nationality is not a problem. Status is not a concern to Him. In fact, He looks for the humble in spirit, the compassionate person and one willing to obey and follow His leading. He brings together those whom He chooses and guides them into His perfect will.

Boaz is considered to be a hero. He saw a need and did not stop to ask questions. He sprang into action with kindness, unselfishness and compassion, giving to Ruth and Naomi renewed hope and stability in place of grief and pain. Boaz, through the pages of history, continues to demonstrate the never ending effects of kindness, decisiveness, courage and respect for his fellowman. Men of any age can be greatly benefited by emulating this man of such noble character.

Naomi, Ruth and Boaz: three outstanding characters. Naomi: the model mother-in-law. Ruth: the model daughter-in-law and friend. Boaz: the gentle yet strong man. I've learned many lessons from them. I've also learned to trust God's providential care. I trust they have taught you some lessons that will help you in your life's journey.

CPSIA information can be obtained
at www.ICGtesting.com
Printed in the USA
LVHW100737060822
725336LV00005B/168